5 favourite worship songs

FLUTE

Kevin Mayhew

We hope you enjoy *25 favourite worship songs for flute*.
Further copies of this and our many other books are available
from your local Kevin Mayhew stockist.

In case of difficulty, please contact the publisher direct by writing to:

The Sales Department
KEVIN MAYHEW LTD
Buxhall
Stowmarket
Suffolk IP14 3BW

Phone 01449 737978
Fax 01449 737834
E-mail info@kevinmayhewltd.com

Please ask for our complete catalogue of outstanding
Piano and Instrumental Music.

First published in Great Britain in 2001 by Kevin Mayhew Ltd.

© Copyright 2001 Kevin Mayhew Ltd.

ISBN 1 84003 759 8
ISMN M 57004 885 4
Catalogue No: 1400281

1 2 3 4 5 6 7 8 9

The music in this book is protected by copyright and may not be reproduced in any way for sale
or private use without the consent of the copyright owner.

Cover design: Jonathan Stroulger
Music setter: Tracy Cook
Proof reader: Marian Hellen

Printed and bound in Great Britain

Contents

	No.		No.
All hail the lamb	1	My lips shall praise you	15
All heaven declares	2	My Lord, what love is this	16
All I once held dear	3	*Once again*	9
Amazing love	16	Peace like a river	17
As the deer pants	4	*Power of your love*	10
Be still, for the presence of the Lord	5	Purify my heart	18
Days of Elijah	21	*Refiner's fire*	18
Father God, I wonder	6	*Restorer of my soul*	15
I need you more	7	*Shine, Jesus, shine*	12
I really want to worship you, my Lord	25	Shout to the lord	14
I stand in awe	24	Thank you for saving me	19
I will offer up my life	8	*The heart of worship*	23
I will sing your praises	6	There is none like you	20
Jesus Christ	9	These are the days	21
Knowing you	3	*This thankful heart*	8
Lord, I come to you	10	We declare your majesty	22
Lord, I lift your name on high	11	When the music fades	23
Lord, the light of your love	12	You are beautiful	24
Majesty	13	*You came from heaven to earth*	11
My Jesus, my Saviour	14	You laid aside your majesty	25

The music on the enclosed CD is in the same order as the music in this book. For example, song no. 4 *As the deer pants* is track no. 4 on the CD.

1 All hail the lamb
Dave Bilbrough

© Copyright 1987 Kingsway's Thankyou Music, P.O. Box 75, Eastbourne, East Sussex BN23 6NW, UK. Used by permission.

2 All heaven declares
Noel and Tricia Richards

© Copyright 1987 Kingsway's Thankyou Music, P.O. Box 75, Eastbourne, East Sussex BN23 6NW, UK. Used by permission.

3 All I once held dear *(Knowing you)*
Graham Kendrick

© Copyright 1993 Make Way Music, P.O. Box 263, Croydon, Surrey CR9 5AP, UK.
International copyright secured. All rights reserved. Used by permission.

4 As the deer pants
Martin J. Nystrom

© Copyright 1983 Restoration Music Ltd. Administered by Sovereign Music UK,
P.O. Box 356, Leighton Buzzard, Bedfordshire LU7 8WP, UK.

5 Be still, for the presence of the Lord
David J. Evans

© Copyright 1986 Kingsway's Thankyou Music, P.O. Box 75, Eastbourne,
East Sussex BN23 6NW, UK. Used by permission.

6 Father God, I wonder *(I will sing your praises)*
Ian Smale

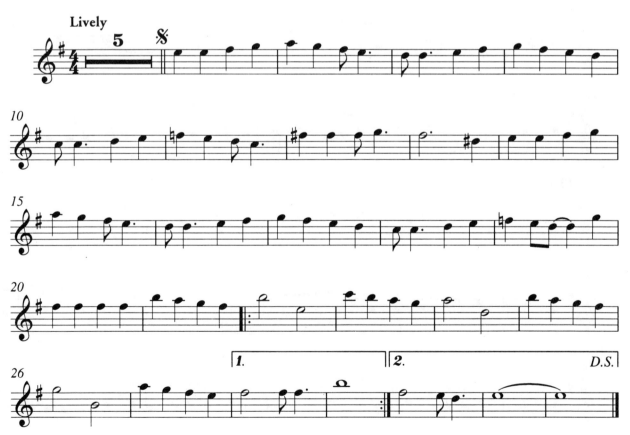

© Copyright 1984 Kingsway's Thankyou Music, P.O. Box 75,
Eastbourne, East Sussex BN23 6NW, UK. Used by permission.

7 I need you more
Lindell Cooley and Bruce Haynes

© Copyright 1996 Integrity's Hosanna! Music. Administered by Kingsway's Thankyou Music, P.O. Box 75, Eastbourne, East Sussex BN23 6NW, UK/Centergy Music. Administered by Integrated Copyright Group, P.O. Box 24149, Nashville, TN 37202, USA. Used by permission.

8 I will offer up my life *(This thankful heart)*
Matt Redman

© Copyright 1994 Kingsway's Thankyou Music, P.O. Box 75,
Eastbourne, East Sussex BN23 6NW, UK. Used by permission.

9 Jesus Christ   *(Once again)*
Matt Redman

© Copyright 1995 Kingsway's Thankyou Music, P.O. Box 75, Eastbourne,
East Sussex, BN23 6NW, UK. Used by permission.

10 Lord, I come to you   *(Power of your love)*
Geoff Bullock

© Copyright 1992 Words Music/Maranatha! Music. Administered by CopyCare,
P.O. Box 77, Hailsham, East Sussex BN27 3EF, UK. (music@copycare.com). Used by permission.

11 Lord, I lift your name on high *(You came from heaven to earth)*
Rick Founds

© Copyright 1989 Maranatha! Music. Administered by CopyCare,
P.O. Box 77, Hailsham, East Sussex BN27 3EF, UK. (music@copycare.com). Used by permission.

12 Lord, the light of your love *(Shine, Jesus, shine)*
Graham Kendrick

© Copyright 1987 Make Way Music, P.O. Box 263, Croydon, Surrey CR9 5AP, UK.
International copyright secured. All rights reserved. Used by permission.

13 Majesty
Jack W. Hayford

© Copyright 1976 Rocksmith Music Inc. Administered by Leosong Copyright Service Ltd,
13 Berners Street, London W1T 3LH, UK. Used by permission.

14 My Jesus, my Saviour   *(Shout to the Lord)*
Darlene Zschech

© Copyright 1993 Darlene Zschech/Hillsong Publishing. Administered by Kingsway's Thankyou Music, P.O Box 75, Eastbourne, East Sussex BN23 6NW, UK. For the UK and Europe. Used by permission.

15 My lips shall praise you   *(Restorer of my soul)*
Noel and Tricia Richards

© Copyright 1991 Kingsway's Thankyou Music, P.O. Box 75, Eastbourne, East Sussex BN23 6NW, UK. Used by permission.

16 My Lord, what love is this   *(Amazing love)*
Graham Kendrick

© Copyright 1989 Make Way Music, P.O. Box 263, Croydon, Surrey CR9 5AP, UK.
International copyright secured. All rights reserved. Used by permission.

17 Peace like a river
John Watson

© Copyright 1989 Ampelos Music. Administered by CopyCare,
P.O. Box 77, Hailsham, East Sussex BN27 3EF, UK. (music@copycare.com). Used by permission.

18 Purify my heart *(Refiner's fire)*
Brian Doerksen

© Copyright 1990 Mercy/Vineyard Publishing. Administered by CopyCare,
P.O. Box 77, Hailsham, East Sussex BN27 3EF, UK. (music@copycare.com). Used by permission.

19 Thank you for saving me
Martin Smith

© Copyright 1993 Curious? Music UK. Administered by Kingsway's Thankyou Music,
P.O. Box 75, Eastbourne, East Sussex BN23 6NW, UK. Worldwide (excl.USA). Used by permission.

20 There is none like you
Lenny LeBlanc

© Copyright 1991 Integrity's Hosanna! Music. Administered by Kingsway's Thankyou Music, P.O. Box 75, Eastbourne, East Sussex BN23 6NW, UK. For the UK only. Used by permission.

21 These are the days *(Days of Elijah)*
Robin Mark

© Copyright 1996 Daybreak Music Ltd, Silverdale Road, Eastbourne, East Sussex BN20 7AB, UK. International copyright secured. All rights reserved. Used by permission.

22 We declare your majesty
Malcolm du Plessis

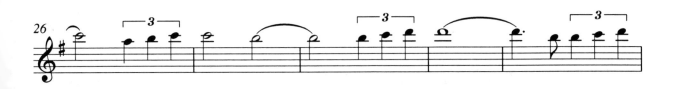

© Copyright 1984 Kingsway's Thankyou Music, P.O. Box 75, Eastbourne,
East Sussex BN23 6NW, UK. Europe only. Used by permission.

23 When the music fades *(The heart of worship)*
Matt Redman

© Copyright 1997 Kingsway's Thankyou Music, P.O. Box 75, Eastbourne,
East Sussex BN23 6NW, UK. Used by permission.

24 You are beautiful *(I stand in awe)*
Mark Altrogge

© Copyright 1987 People of Destiny International. Administered by CopyCare,
P.O. Box 77, Hailsham, East Sussex BN27 3EF, UK. (music@copycare.com). Used by permission.

25 You laid aside your majesty
(I really want to worship you, my Lord)

Noel Richards

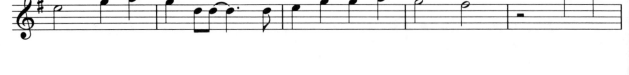

© Copyright 1985 Kingsway's Thankyou Music, P.O. Box 75, Eastbourne, East Sussex BN23 6NW, UK. Used by permission.

Also available from Kevin Mayhew . . .

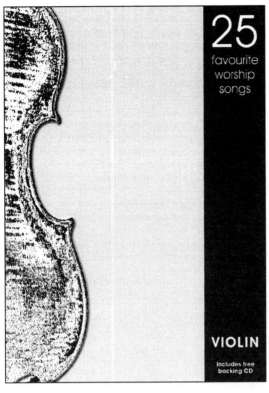

◀ 25 favourite worship songs - VIOLIN
1400280

25 favourite worship songs - CLARINET ▶
1400288

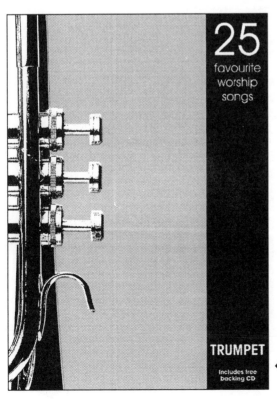

◀ 25 favourite worship songs - TRUMPET
1400289